John Sinclair

Reflexions on the expediency of increasing the present number of the representatives of the people

John Sinclair

Reflexions on the expediency of increasing the present number of the representatives of the people

ISBN/EAN: 9783337224622

Printed in Europe, USA, Canada, Australia, Japan

Cover: Foto ©Suzi / pixelio.de

More available books at **www.hansebooks.com**

REFLEXIONS

ON THE

EXPEDIENCY

OF

INCREASING

THE

PRESENT NUMBER

OF THE

REPRESENTATIVES

OF

THE PEOPLE.

BY

JOHN SINCLAIR, Esq. M. P.

" Nous reſſemblons à ceux qui habitent des maiſons qui leur ſont
" échues en heritage, et qui, au riſque d'en être écraſés, n'y
" veulent rien changer, pour ne pas toucher a l'ouvrage de leur
" peres, comme ſi c'etoit manquer a la veneration qui leur eſt
" dûe, que de rétablir ou de perfectionner ce qu'ils ont fait.
" Il eſt certain en effet que l'edifice de notre republique s'af-
" faiſe par ſon propre poids; & rien peut-être ne ſera compa-
" rable un jours à ſes malheurs, s'il eſt vrai qu'il n'eſt rien de
" pire, que la corruption de ce qui eſt excellent." Dans la
Preface de La Voix libre du Citoyen : ou, Obſervations ſur le
Gouvernment de Pologne. Par STANISLAS, Roi de Pologne.

LONDON:

Printed for T. CADELL, in the Strand.

M. DCC. LXXXII.

[Price ONE SHILLING.]

ADVERTISEMENT.

DURING the laſt ſeſſion of parliament, the author of this tract took the liberty of ſtating to the public a plan of parliamentary reform, in a work entitled " Lucubrations during a ſhort Receſs ". Though the principles which it contained appeared to him juſt in themſelves, analogous to the Britiſh conſtitution, and not difficult to execute, he found, with regret, that many worthy and able men were of opinion that it went too far ; and ſoon afterwards it appeared (when a committee was propoſed for inquiring into the preſent ſtate of the repreſentation of the people) that the houſe was not ripe for an alteration of ſuch extent and importance. The neceſſity of ſome conſtitutional reform is, however, generally acknowledged. It only remains, therefore, to diſcover what plan is the beſt entitled to receive the ſanction of both houſes of parliament, the approbation of the crown, and the concurrence of the people. With a view of contributing to ſo deſirable a diſcovery, the following Reflexions were compoſed.

The

The author's principal object is, to support an idea originally attributed to the late Earl of Chatham, of adding a certain number of representatives to the different counties, leaving the other parts of the constitution subject only to such partial alterations as took place in respect to Shoreham and to Cricklade. He is still inclined to think, that the constitution of Great Britain ought to resemble the sacred galley of Athens, into which new beams were occasionally inserted, and the old and rotten ones taken away. But if wiser and abler men are of opinion that the vessel ought to be still more cautiously handled; and that from years it has been reduced to a state too feeble to undergo a thorough repair, or to suffer even a single plank to be removed; for one, he is willing to submit his judgment to greater experience and abilities, trusting, at the same time, that something will be done, *sufficient to preserve so dear a* PALLADIUM *from running to total ruin and decay.*

REFLEXIONS, &c.

NO queftion has divided legiflators and ftatefmen more, than how far it is expedient to permit any material alteration in the government of a ftate.

Againft innovations, it has been generally urged, that when once a nation is accuftomed to alter its political regulations, even on grounds apparently fufficient, that it is impoffible to fay how far the defire of change may be carried; and that it may be gradually led from ftep to ftep, until it has totally loft fight of every veftige of its ancient conftitution. The moft dangerous laws, it has been faid, may be propofed, under the moft fpecious pretences; nor can the ableft ftatefman forefee the remote confequences of the moft minute alteration. However plaufible fuch arguments may at firft fight appear, yet they evidently prove too much, and muft be rejected when brought as fufficient grounds to eftablifh every poffible fpe-

cies

cies of abufe, which may creep into the conftitution of a country.

It may be granted, that alterations in government ought to be very cautioufly admitted, when any legiflator has been appointed to form a new conftitution, and has compofed one whole, in which each part is fo intimately connected with the other, that by injuring the fmalleft wheel, the whole fabric may be deftroyed. Such was the cafe at Sparta, and in other ancient republics; but it will be difficult to prove, that we ever had a Solon or a Lycurgus in this ifland, to whofe fole wifdom, penetration and experience we are indebted, for the government which we poffefs.

It may alfo be granted, that if any alterations which have crept into a ftate, are only an extenfion of the firft principles of its original conftitution, and have not tended to fap the foundation of any of thofe pillars on which it was originally built, that a conftitution thus formed ought likewife to be accounted a hallowed fane, never in future to be fubjected to rafh and wanton violation.

But

But furely no one can pretend to fay, that
the alterations which have taken place in
the government of this ifland (at leaft with
refpect to extending the right of fending reprefentatives to parliament) have been an
extenfion of the original principles on which
that council was founded. Parliaments
were eftablifhed as a check upon the power
of the crown, and with a view of preventing
the executive branch of the government
from becoming defpotic and tyrannical.
Whereas almoft every partial augmentation
of the number of reprefentatives, fince the
reign of Edward the Firft, was calculated
for a very different purpofe. The additions
to the number of members, when Wales was
incorporated with England, and when the
union with Scotland took place, were neceffary. New citizens muft have new reprefentatives in every free ftate. But what advantage could be gained, except increafing the
influence of the crown, by the number of
paltry boroughs which, fince the reign of
that monarch, were invefted with parliamentary privileges ?

I am

I am alfo ready to confefs, that if this nation had every reafon to be fatisfied with its prefent fituation; if it were happy at home, and refpected abroad; if its neighbours courted its friendfhip, and if its enemies trembled at its wrath; in that cafe, that the fyftems of political projectors ought to be very cautioufly liftened to. But is that our cafe at prefent? Have we any reafon to be afraid, that any conftitutional alteration can reduce us from fplendor to mifery, or from greatnefs to contempt? On the contrary, the only profpect we have of enabling our pofterity to rival the power and fortune of our anceftors, is to leave them in legacy a fimilar conftitution to that which thefe anceftors gloried to enjoy.

There would alfo be fome reafon to object to any material alteration, were it not evident, that all our public misfortunes may be afcribed to the dangerous abufes, which have been fuffered to take root in the government of this country. The conduct of minifters, and of thofe they employed, both in the commencement and profecution of

6   the

the American war, had become fo unpopu-
lar, long before it was given up, that there
is great reafon to doubt, whether it could
have been at all commenced, much lefs fo
long perfevered in, had not a parliament
ftood between the crown and the people, to
deaden the oppofition of the one, and to
countenance the unfortunate fyftem which
the other had adopted. Whereas had the
wifhes of the people for conciliatory meafures with America fooner taken place, we
fhould not at this time have been abjectly
fupplicating for peace at the hands, if not
at the feet of our enemies.

If our government, therefore, was not
eftablifhed at once, but has been fubject to
almoft perpetual fluctuation; if any partial
alterations which have taken place, have
been contrary to thofe principles, on which
parliamentary councils were originally
founded; if the nation is reduced to a
ftate, which gives it little reafon to be
afraid of the poffible dangers which may
arife from material innovations; and if the
prefent conftitution of parliament has proved
inimical to the public profperity; where is
the

[6]

the harm of propofing, or of carrying into execution, fuch fyftems of reform, as feem to be eſſentially neceſſary for the future happinefs of the ſtate?

There are three circumſtances in the nature and conſtitution of parliament, to which it is neceſſary at this time to advert, as from all of them the influence of the crown has been conſiderably increaſed; namely, *the places* which have acquired a right of fending reprefentatives; *the manner* in which thofe reprefentatives have been elected; and *the number* of which they do at preſent confiſt, when aſſembled together.

It is univerfally acknowledged, that from the partiality of particular monarchs, and from other circumſtances, which it is by no means neceſſary to dwell upon, a number of *places* in the kingdom have acquired the right of fending reprefentatives to parliament; and confequently have obtained a weight in the legiſlature, to which they are not in any refpect entitled, except *merely in confeʒuence of poſſeſſion:* And it is certain, that the original idea of parliament would

be

be reftored, were the rights and franchifes of a certain number of thefe places tranf-ferred from them to fome of the more im-portant diftricts in the kingdom. But as every plan of that nature would remove, it is faid, fome old conftitutional landmarks, it has not met with fo general an approba-tion as perhaps it was entitled to expect.

The manner in which the members of the different boroughs in the kingdom were elected, by permitting every one to vote, however dependent they were on the exe-cutive branch of the legiflature, enabled the crown alfo to acquire an influence in parlia-ment, which undoubtedly was not originally intended. Some late regulations, however, pro-hibiting the votes of the revenue officers, &c. have tended materially to remove the confe-quences of this evil. But every one muft perceive, that though fuch alterations are beneficial, yet they are of too partial a na-ture to prove an effectual means of enabling the real friends of the people, efficacioufly to oppofe any pernicious fyftem which the crown in future may adopt.

It

It only remains, therefore, to be confidered, how far it is poffible, by increafing *the prefent number* of the reprefentatives of the people, to difable the crown, by means of any revenue or influence which it is likely to poffefs, ever to gain a fubfervient majority in the lower affembly; and whether, in confequence of fuch an addition, the wifhes of the people might not always be certain of obtaining fo formidable a fupport in parliament, againft any improper meafures of government, as to give them, on every fuch occafion, a certainty of fuccefs.

It is well known, that the members of the Englifh houfe of commons were not always fo numerous as they are at prefent. In the year 1446, they did not exceed 274, of which 200 reprefented the different cities and boroughs in the kingdom.

But the crown having affumed to itfelf the power of creating boroughs *ad libitum*, and finding every day that it became more and more neceffary to have the fupport and countenance of parliament in the government

ment of the state, made ufe of its creative prerogative, in granting to a number of infignificant villages, parliamentary privileges, in hopes, by fuch means, of always having a confiderable fhare of the members of the legiflature devoted to it. From hence originated the undue influence of the crown among the reprefentatives of the people; and thence it has become neceffary, if no other means of reform can be adopted, that fuch an addition fhould be made to the prefent members of the houfe of commons, as may counterbalance the weight that has been thrown into the fcale of the crown. An addition of 50 reprefentatives to the moft important diftricts in England, in the opinion of the ableft ftatefmen of modern times, has been fuppofed neceffary to form a fufficient counterpoife. By fuch an increafe, with 5 for Scotland, the number it is entitled to expect *, the houfe would amount to 613 members; 100 more than it had prior to the union.

---

* Scotland, by the articles of the union, is entitled to one twelfth part of the whole reprefentation in parliament, which, without entering into fractions, 50 is of 613, as 45 is of 558, the number of which the houfe at prefent confifts.

The

The firft objection that might be adduced againft fuch a plan is, that the houfe is already fufficiently numerous, and that fo large an addition would render it unfit for the purpofes of deliberation and debate. This is an objection which appeared, on a former occafion, fufficiently plaufible to the author of this tract, until having had an opportunity of examining it more fully, he has found fufficient grounds to alter his opinion : for it is fingular, that both in ancient and in modern times, SIX HUNDRED feems to have been confidered as the proper number of which the fenate of an extenfive fociety ought to be compofed.

At Heraclia, we are informed by Ariftotle that the powers of government, inftead of being in the hands of a few, was vefted in 600 *.

At Athens, though its fenate originally confifted of only 400 members, yet 200 were afterwards added, when its empire came to be increafed †.

---

* Polit. lib. v. cap. 6.
† Bodin de Repub. lib. iii.

The

The oldeſt of the nobility were ſenators for life in the republic of Carthage, without any reſtriction *; but it is conjectured that 600 was the uſual number to which it amounted.

The ſenate of Rome increaſed with the greatneſs of its empire, and from 100 was augmented to above 1000 by Cæſar the Dictator †. So great a multitude, however, having been found inconvenient, the ſenate was again reduced by Auguſtus to 600 (which ſeems indeed to have been the number of which it conſiſted, during the moſt flouriſhing period of the republic): And hence, in the words of Sueton, that emperor reſtored it " admodum priſtinum et ſplendorem " ‡.

The ancient republic of Marſeilles was particularly famous for a wiſe and well-conſtituted government; and among other

---

* Alex. ab. Alex. vol. i. p. 1009.
† Chapman on the Roman Senate.
‡ Suet. Octav. c. xxxv.

parti-

particulars handed down to us refpecting that ftate, we are informed that it alfo boafted of having 600 fenators *.

At Venice alfo, the fons of the nobility, fince the year 1289, are nobles, and form what is called there the Great Council. The number of thofe capacitated by age to be the members of it, in general amounted to 12 or 1300; but as one half of them refide in other places, that council alfo is ufually compofed of about 600 members †.

At Genoa alfo, from 6 to 700 public councellors are entrufted with the government of the ftate ‡.

But if, in other free and well-governed ftates, fuch a number as 600 fenators was not confidered to be too numerous a body

---

* Alex. ab. Alexan. vol. i. p. 1009.

† See Addifon's Travels, p. 63, 64. Miffon's Travels, vol. ii. p. 476 & 477.

‡ Miffon's Travels, vol. iii. p. 270 & 375.

At Cretona there were 1000 fenators. See Bayle's Dict. vol. iii. p. 614. Note G. article Pythagoras.

for

for the purpofes of ferious inveftigation, far
lefs is there any reafon to confider that as an
objection in this country; the commons of
Great Britain not being compofed of the
citizens of one particular town, but of individuals fent from every diftrict of an extenfive kingdom, however diftant and remote.
Their attendance, therefore, cannot be fo
regular, nor confequently their number fo
inconvenient, as if they were conftant inhabitants of that town in which the council
affembled; more efpecially as the houfe
has ever confifted of perfons engaged in a
variety of different profeffions, who are
often bufied about their own private affairs,
and are not very urgently or frequently
compelled to attendance in parliament.

Before the queftion of number is difmiffed,
it may be proper to remark, that when,
with a view of putting an end to the trou-
bles in America, it was propofed to admit
the inhabitants of that country to a fhare in
the parliament of Great Britain, that the
idea was countenanced by that able ftatefman Mr. Grenville, who was no friend to

rafh

rafh and dangerous innovations *. It is certain, that a confiderable number of American reprefentatives muft have been admitted into the houfe of commons; and as no objection was urged at that time on the ground of number, no reafon can be given why it fhould be made a handle of on the prefent occafion.

In the fecond place, it may be objected, that fuch an addition would not fufficiently reduce the influence of the crown in parliament, which undoubtedly at this time is the great object of all conftitutional innovations. But before it is attempted to remove this objection, it will be neceffary to explain the fpecific nature of the alterations that are propofed.

The reprefentatives of the people in parliament, are either fent by the different

* See particularly the Prefent State of the Nation, either written by him, or under his immediate direction, 2d edit. p. 80, &c. where, among other things, this refpectable fenator obferves, that the number of electors has become too fmall in proportion to the whole people.

towns

towns and boroughs, or by the different
counties in the kingdom; and though, for
many reasons, the reprefentatives of the
landed property in the kingdom (which the
county members only can properly be accounted) ought to have at leaft an equal
fhare in the third branch of the legiflature,
and actually had about one third in the reign
of Henry the Sixth, yet now 128 out of
558 members is the whole number they can
boaft of, including the counties in Wales
and Scotland, and the members for the two
univerfities. If, therefore, any increafe is
to be made to the prefent number of reprefentatives, they ought furely to be diftri-
buted among the different fhires in the kingdom, and the two cities of London and
Weftminfter, whofe population and wealth
feem to entitle them to an addition of two
members each.

It has been urged by fome, if any alteration were to take place, that it would be
neceffary to attend very particularly to the
intereft of the great manufacturing towns of
Manchefter, Birmingham, &c. From whatever the author has feen of parliament, he is
inclined

inclined to be of a very different opinion. He has uniformly obferved almoft every member of the houfe willing to fupport any reafonable plan that could be fuggefted, for the advantage of our commercial or manu- facturing interefts ; and in every queftion in which the towns of Mancbefter and of Bir- mingham were concerned, the members for the counties of Lancafter and of Warwick, were as eager and zealous in the matter, as if their only conftituents had been in thofe towns. The interference of county mem- bers muft always have more weight with the houfe, than the reprefentatives of any town, however refpectable : and as the members for the county would not confider themfelves under any great obligation to attend to the intereft of a place that had others more particularly connected with it, it is probable that the towns in queftion would rather lofe than gain by the alteration ; nor could it be of any advantage to them to have their induftry even occafionally dif- turbed, by the tumults of an election.

If the addition that is propofed were not confined to the counties and to the capital,

it

it would be very difficult, if not impoffible, to determine with propriety, among the different pretenfions of thofe towns, which would put in their claim for a fhare in the legiflature; fome pleading their having no reprefentatives; others, that they had not their proportion; fome arguing from their wealth, others from their population, and perhaps fome from their antiquity. Whereas, in fact, as the wealthieft citizens of all great towns are poffeffed of votes in the neighbouring counties, with the increafe of county reprefentatives, the influence of thofe towns in parliament muft neceffarily be augmented.

The wealth and number of inhabitants in the two counties of Yorkfhire and Middlefex, feem to entitle them to two additional reprefentatives each, as well as London and Weftminfter. The remaining 42 members might be given at the rate of one each to thofe counties in England and Wales, by whom the land tax is paid in the greateft proportion. Some difference undoubtedly there is between various counties in refpect to fize, opulence and population. But it is impoffible to enter minutely into fuch di-

ftinctions,

ftinctions, nor can it be of material confequence to the public, or indeed to any particular county, whether it fends its exact
proportion to parliament. The great object
being that an addition fhould be made to
the prefent reprefentatives of the people,
confifting of a defcription of men, who
would not probably come into parliament
with views meerly of ambition, or of per-
fonal advantage.

The following fketch will at one glance
explain to the reader to what counties it is
proper that an addition of one reprefentative
fhould be given; and if it fhould be the
opinion of the houfe that Effex, Kent, Nor-
folk, &c. fhould have two members, what
counties muft be cut off in confequence of
fuch an alteration.

Counties.		Land Tax.
Effex	—	— £.89,390
Kent	—	— 86,553
Norfolk	—	— 84,306
Devonfhire	-	— 82,583
Suffolk	—	— 73,506
Lincolnfhire	-	— 71,907
		Somer-

Counties.			Land Tax.
Somerfetfhire	-	—	70,473
Surrey	—	—	66,132
Suffex	—	—	60,091
Wiltfhire	-	—	51,657
Southamptonfhire		—	49,359
Northamptonfhire		—	47,660
Bucks	—	—	47,142
Gloucefterfhire		—	45,942
Hertfordfhire		—	42,371
Berks	-	—	40,843
Warwickfhire		—	39,789
Oxfordfhire	-	—	35,651
Leicefterfhire		—	34,685
Worcefterfhire		—	33,582
Dorfetfhire	-	—	33,071
Cambridgefhire		—	32,732
Cornwall	-	—	31,943
Shropfhire	-	—	29,056
Chefhire	-	—	28,598
Bedfordfhire	-	—	28,554
Nottinghamfhire		—	27,276
Staffordfhire	-	—	27,120
Derbyfhire	-	—	24,993
Lancafhire	-	—	20,989
Herefordfhire	-	—	20,409
Huntingdonfhire		—	15,497

Northum-

Counties.		Land Tax.
Northumberland	—	14,548
Durham —	—	10,597
Monmouthfhire	—	9,812
Glamorganfhire	—	7,906
Denbigh —	—	6,800
Montgomery	—	5,852
Rutland —	—	5,525
Cumberland	—	3,713
Pembroke -	—	3,172
Weftmoreland	—	3,045

It has been already ftated, that if fifty
were to be added to the different reprefentatives in England, that an addition of
5 muft be given to the northern part of the
ifland, of which 3 would indifputably fall
to the fhare of certain counties in that part
of the kingdom who, contrary to every principle of this conftitution, are only reprefented every fecond parliament. The city
of Glafgow, the magnitude of whofe trade
is well known, and which, unlike Birmingham and Manchefter, at prefent goes
through all the forms of election, (in confequence of the privilege which it enjoys in
connection with three other boroughs of
fending

fending a member to parliament) is well entitled to a reprefentative for itfelf, and no
one probably will object to the Univerfities
of Scotland having one reprefentative in the
great council of the nation *.

Having thus explained the particulars of
the propofed plan, it may be obferved, that
any one who candidly confiders the hiftory
of parliament for fome years paft muft be
fenfible, that if fuch a body had been added
to the reprefentatives of the people fome
years ago, in all probability a great fhare of
the misfortunes which this country has ex-
perienced would have been prevented : for
it cannot be fuppofed that a parliament fo

* It may not be improper to take this opportunity of remarking, that very unreafonable prejudices are entertained
in England refpecting the fhare which Scotland enjoys in
the legiflature. It is faid that Scotland ought to have members and peers in parliament in proportion only to the land
tax which it pays, as if men were not every bit as neceffary
for a ftate as money, and as if it were of no advantage to
England to have its fifter kingdom a friend and not a foe.
The proper reply to fuch reafoning is, look to Holland, and
there you will fee that Overyffel has an equal fhare with the
province of Holland in the general affembly of the States,
though the firft contributes at the rate of 35,711, whilft the
other pays no lefs a fum than 583,090 guilders. See Wil-
liams's North. Gov. Vol. i. p. 61, 63.

conftituted

conftituted would have fuffered the fatal in-
activity of the late minifters at the commencement of the American difpute, or the
feries of accumulated blunders, by which
the profecution of it was diftinguifhed.
Had fuch an alteration alfo taken place, the
conteft between the two political parties
would have been much fooner brought to a
decifion. It is well known that the late
adminiftration was nearly overturned in confequence of the fuccefs which attended the
memorable motion made on the 5th of
April, 1779, refpecting the influence of the
crown : And if one can judge how additional
reprefentatives for counties would have voted
from the manner in which thofe who were
fent actually did vote, that motion muft
have been carried by a ftill greater majority.
Nay, there is reafon to imagine, that the
change in his majefty's councils would have
taken place much fooner even in this parliament, had the plan in queftion exifted
fome time ago. On Sir James Lowther's
motion, on the 12th of December, 1781,
there were prefent 68 members, to whofe
places of reprefentation the 50 additional
members in England would probably be
given.

given. Of thefe 54 voted for Sir James
Lowther's motion, and only 14 againft it:
to reafon, therefore, from analogy, it may
be faid, that of the 50 that would have been
added, in all probability, one-fifth would
have voted againft the motion, and the remaining four-fifths for it. The addition of
40 members to the one fide, and of only 10
to the other, would undoubtedly have ended
the conteft before the Chriftmas holidays *.
Without entering at all into any comparifon
between the two parties, either in refpect of
ability or of zeal for the public fervice, it
will probably be allowed, that fince a change
was to take place in his majefty's councils,
it has proved unfortunate in the event that
it was not fooner effected, whilft the principles of conciliation which one party pro-
feffed had fome chance of being fuccefsful,
and before the feeble and irritating exertions
of the other had totally eftranged America

---

* Far lefs would the fame addition have prevented the
fuccefs of General Conway's motion on the 27th of Feb.
1782. There were prefent then 78 members in the predi-
cament above ftated, of which 68 voted for the motion, and
only 12 againft it: by the fame mode of reafoning, therefore, the motion would have been carried by a ftill greater
majority than it actually was.

from

from us, and incorporated her with our neighbours. At any rate, it would be difficult to prove, had such a plan been established, that our present situation could have been worse.

There being therefore ample grounds to imagine that such an addition would be a sufficient check upon any inordinate influence of the crown, it is also probable that it would be attended with this advantage, namely, that of preventing unreasonable, dangerous or interested factions in the state : a violent spirit of party, which is too apt to degenerate into faction, would be not a little checked by the superintendance of 55 additional senators, who, in all probability, would not enlist under the banners of either the minister or of his opponents. Indeed, with the uncertainty what part they would take, it would be in vain to think of acquiring consequence by forming a party of 50 or even 100 members, when the whole assembly consisted of 600 ; many of whom would not constantly attend their place in parliament, and consequently, whose tempers and dispositions could not possibly be
known ;

known: Whereas, if any fyftem apparently
dangerous was purfued, which it was neceffary for the nation at large to check and to
controul, it would fcarcely be poffible, by
any arts or influence, to fecure a majority of
fo large an affembly fo admirably conftituted.

Another material advantage attending
fuch an addition to the number of members
is, that a feat in parliament would not become, in an interefted view, of fuch confequence to any individual; and that the
houfe would probably for the future confift
of only two defcriptions of men; one of
which would be determined never to accept
of any office under the crown; and the
other anxious, by a painful and laborious
attention to public affairs, to qualify themfelves for public employments: not to omit
mentioning, that until the efficacy of this
remedy was fairly tried, the warmeft friends
to annual or triennial parliaments would not
think it neceffary to propofe again to have
recourfe to fuch dangerous experiments.

E   The

The more that county members alfo are
increafed, the greater reafon will there be
to expect, that a general fpirit of improvement will prevail in the country at large.
Thofe who are poffeffed of confiderable
landed eftates, are every day refiding more
and more in the capital, or in little villas in
its neighbourhood ; and the country would
be almoft totally deferted by individuals of
that defcription, were it not that many are
defirous of preferving the intereft of their
refpective families, in the different diftricts
they are connected with. The more that
county members, therefore, are increafed,
the greater inducement will there be for a
number of wealthy and opulent people to
refide, at leaft occafionally, in the country,
to fpend a larger proportion of their income
there, and to pay greater attention to the
cultivation and the improvement of their
eftates ; and of whatever importance com-
merce and manufactures are defervedly
efteemed, yet agriculture ought to be accounted the real bafis of public profperity.

I know that many urge it as an objection
to any increafe of county reprefentatives,

that

that it will tend to augment the power of the peerage in the houfe of commons, which they imagine is already too great. Of all the objections to fuch a meafure, this feems to have the leaft foundation. It is well known, that during the late conteft, a large majority of the houfe of peers were attached to Lord North's adminiftration; and yet, on General Conway's motion on the 27th of February laft, of 78 county members who voted on that occafion, only 12 are fuppofed to have given their voice in favour of the minifter. Ariftocratical influence may poffibly prevail in fome particular counties, but the evil is far from being general; nor indeed would there be great reafon to lament, that the *opinion* of any refpectable individual, who wifely and liberally expended his annual income in a manner which entitled him to the efteem and confidence of his neighbours, fhould have fome weight in the diftrict where he refides.

Laftly, though fuch an addition will naturally diminifh the importance of each individual in parliament, yet at the fame time it will not only render the houfe itfelf a

more

more refpectable affembly, but will alfo en-
able it to judge more fully regarding the
wifhes of its conftituents, and the interefts
of the public. We are told of the Roman
fenate, that Sylla, finding its influence had
become inconfiderable, in confequence of
the fmallnefs of its number, reduced by
profcriptions and civil wars, found it neceffary to make an addition of 300 fenators at
once * ; and if the number was not found
inconvenient, we have reafon to believe,
from the opinion which Ariftotle has given,
as well as from higher authority, that a
multitude of councellors is not inconfiftent
with the fafety of a ftate. As the able
ftatefman and philofopher alluded to well
obferves, fince public fuppers exceed thofe
which are given at one perfon's private expence, fo many, when joined together, are
better qualified for fupreme power than a
few; for though not one of the multitude
affembled together may be fit for power
himfelf, yet every individual of which it is
compofed, brings in his fhare of wifdom and
ability †.

<hr/>

* See Chapman on the Roman Senate.
† Polit. lib. iii. c. 11.

If,

If, in confequence of thefe, and of other reafons which will naturally occur to the reader, the addition above propofed to the prefent reprefentatives of the people, fhould be thought a defirable meafure, the proper mode of difcovering the fenfe of parliament refpecting it, would be, to move a refolution in the houfe of commons, to the following purport.

" Resolved, That it is the opinion of " this houfe, that an addition to the prefent " number of the reprefentatives of the peo- " ple, not exceeding fifty for that part of " Great Britain called England (including " the principality of Wales), and of five for " that part of Great Britain called Scotland, " is a meafure expedient in itfelf, and ne- " ceffary to be adopted at this time, as a " means of rendering the reprefentation of " the people more complete, and of enabling " parliament more fully to know the fenfe " and wifhes of its conftituents."

By moving a fpecific propofition, the greater part of thofe objections which were made to the appointment of a committee

4 .. for

for inquiring into the prefent ftate of the reprefentation of the people, would be done away: and furely if any plan, entitled to meet with the approbation of the houfe, could at once be propofed, it would be better than entering into that *mare magnum,* which a certain learned lord fo ably and vehemently oppofed.

But probably this meafure would not of itfelf be fufficient to fatisfy the wifhes of the people. To make the conftitution fufficiently perfect, it would be neceffary gradually to alter the ftrange and abfurd manner in which the reprefentatives of the different boroughs in the kingdom are generally chofen, and occafionally to increafe the number of voters in fuch places, as has been done in the cafes of Shoreham and of Cricklade. As fuch alterations, however, ought to be gradually effected; at leaft, as fome objections might be made to infringe upon eftablifhed franchifes, without proof of their being improperly made ufe of; it might be fufficient to have the following order added to the ftanding orders of the houfe.

" OR-

" ORDERED, That fuch committees as
" are appointed to confider petitions refpect-
" ing any controverted borough election,
" fhall in future inquire into the mode of
" election in the place to which the petition
" relates ; and fhall report the fame, with
" their opinions thereupon, to the houfe."

No member of the houfe, who has ever
fat on fuch a committee, will object to this
important point being fully afcertained by
the exprefs orders of the houfe.

Such is the plan of reform, which the
author of this tract ventures to recommend
to the attention of parliament, and of the
public. It is unneceffary, however, for him
to come to any refolution with regard to
making the motions above-mentioned, until
it is known what fteps are intended to be
taken by adminiftration in general ; and in
particular, by that refpectable fenator, who
has taken the lead in queftions of this nature. The firft motion refpecting an increafe of members, feems to belong to that
right honourable perfon almoft by hereditary
right ; and no man can be lefs defirous of
prevent-

preventing fuch an important undertaking
from being continued in the hands of one,
fo peculiarly well qualified for carrying it
through with fuccefs.

Various reafons, however, may be affigned, why no time fhould be loft in taking
the fenfe of parliament refpecting fuch a reform; and why the prefent ought to be accounted the happy moment, that is likely
to be crowned with the greateft blefling that
this country can defire.

The character of the fovereign now upon
the throne, and the certainty that no juft
and reafonable plan, for the purpofe of im-
proving the conftitution, will receive any
obftruction or difcountenance from him, is
a circumftance which, were it at all neceffary, the author could dwell upon with pleafure. Indeed a monarch poffeffed of his
experience and good fenfe muft be fenfible,
that any improper influence of the crown in
parliament, can never be truly advantageous
to the perfon who poffeffes that dignity:
for no enterprize worthy a great king can be
fuccefsfully attempted, however much fanc-
tioned

tioned by parliament, if it is undertaken in oppofition to the general fenfe and wifhes of the people.

Such a plan alfo is certain of every affift-ance that can be required, from the members of the prefent adminiftration. They have pledged themfelves to fupport fome meafure of that nature, with all their talents and authority; and their weight in parliament, though great from the magnitude of the firft, cannot be diminifhed by the poffeffion of the latter.

The prefent temper of the members of the houfe of commons, affords much reafon to imagine, that the plan above propofed would meet with the general approbation of that affembly. Their minds feem to be at laft open to the neceffity of fuch a ftep; and as it is a matter in which that houfe alone is concerned, it is rather improbable that it could poffibly meet with any fuccefsful oppofition in the upper houfe of parliament.

As to the people at large, if the plan above ftated were to fucceed, all parties

F   among

among them, whatever their opinions might
be refpecting conftitutional reforms, would
probably be fatisfied. The friends to innovation would be happy that they have gained
fo much; its foes, that they have loft fo
little.

The author cannot conclude, without
earneftly entreating thofe whofe bufinefs it
is more peculiarly to watch over the fafety
and intereft of the public, not to confider
this as a matter which may be trifled with,
or laid afide. The general principles of
civil liberty are at prefent well known in
almoft every corner of the kingdom. The
neceffity of adopting fome conftitutional reform, is an idea prevalent throughout the
nation; and, in particular, pervades the beft
and moft induftrious part of the community.
Our minifters and others, therefore, may
be affured, that if fomething is not done to
fatisfy the people that their ancient government is reftored, no penal ftatutes will be
fufficient to retain them within the circle
of this ifland : they will migrate; America
will open, with expanded arms, an afylum
for

for their reception; and the peace that muft foon take place, will prove more de-ftructive to the wealth, the induftry, and the population of Great Britain, than the fatal war, the exiftence of which we had fuch ample grounds to mourn over, and to lament.

A P P E N D I X.

A VERY ingenious author having done me the honour of writing an anfwer to the plan of reform formerly fubmitted to the public, in a tract which he has entitled " A Letter to the Author of the Lucubrations during a fhort Recefs," it would be extremely improper to publifh any other performance upon the fame fubject, without paying attention to the obfervations which he has made; particularly as he has fallen into fome miftakes, refpecting the principles which he afcribes to me; and as there are certain points, in which I muft ftill take the liberty of differing from him.

He begins with an obfervation (Letter, p. 5) and indeed is perpetually recurring to it, that the principle on which the plan alluded to is founded, was that of equal reprefentation. Nay we are told (p. 6) that it is obvious " that the principle of equal " reprefentation *is the only one* applied to " that reform : " whereas fuch an idea never
entered

entered into the author's thoughts. He was indeed defirous of feeing a plan of reprefentation MORE COMPLETE than it is at prefent; but he was far from carrying his ideas to that fummit of theoretical purity, for which other writers are more entitled to be attacked, if they are to blame, to whom indeed the greater part of the reafoning contained in this Letter more particularly applies.

But it may be afked, If you do not proceed on the principles of equal reprefentation, how comes it to pafs that you propofe to annihilate in part, or in whole, thofe boroughs only which elect their members by the feweft number of voters?

The principal reafon which led the author to purfue that line, was this, that no borough could fuffer amputation, without fome violence being done to the rights, the franchifes, and the interefts of the electors in the borough; confequently, the fewer voters there were in any disfranchifed borough, on the rights of fewer citizens any infringement would be made: and as compenfation was propofed to be given them,

for

for the privileges of which they were deprived, it was much easier to divide such compensation among a small, than among a numerous body. Besides, the real or supposed number of voters is far from being the only principle of the plan contained in the Lucubrations: for in p. 35 it is observed, that either total non-existence (by which is meant, almost a complete want of electors) or the county in which any borough is situated having an undue proportion in the legislature, are the only two just grounds for cutting off the entire franchises of a borough; and p. 34, that those boroughs only are proposed to be annihilated, which are either the most insignificant in themselves, or have been the most recently invested with parliamentary privileges. Nay Winchester, Salisbury, Andover, &c. though their representatives are elected by very few voters, are expressly excepted, in consequence of their being towns of considerable size; and consequently entitled, from their wealth, population, &c. to a share in the legislature. The principle of equal representation, therefore, in the plan contained in the Lucubrations, was so combined and interwoven with others so capable of correcting

recting its defects, that it cannot juftly be
accounted the fingle pillar on which that
fabric was reared.

It may not be improper to take this opportunity of remarking, that the writer in
queftion feems to entertain an erroneous
opinion, when he afferts (p. 6) " that the
" privilege of fending members to parlia-
" ment, conferred at different times upon
" cities and boroughs, can never be confi-
" dered but as local privileges, upon the
" fame footing with other privileges and
" immunities, which were varied in their
" circumftances, at the good pleafure of the
" prince who granted them ". That the
fovereign did affume the right of granting
parliamentary privileges to particular places,
is too well known to be denied : but there
is a claufe in an act of parliament, in the
reign of that arbitrary monarch Henry the
Eighth, which is worth reciting ; not only
as it proves that the king was not entitled
to make any innovation in the rights of
boroughs, in virtue of his own prerogative
(as is commonly imagined) or indeed legally
to grant new privileges of that nature ; but
alfo as it forms a very fingular and impor-

tant

tant precedent of parliament disfranchising boroughs, when substantial reasons occurred for taking such a measure. The clause alluded to is to the following purport.

" Provided always, and be it enacted by
" the authority aforesaid, that forasmuch as
" there be divers and many small boroughs
" and towns corporate within the said do-
" minion of Wales, whereof many have
" their commencement by grants from the
" lords marchers, and some by other means,
" our said sovereign lord shall from henceforth,
" *by virtue of his act*, have full power and
" authority, by his letters patent, to be en-
" rolled in his grace's high court of chan-
" cery, at any time within seven years here-
" after next ensuing, to the end of this pre-
" sent parliament, *to repel, annihilate and*
" *dissolve* such and as many of the said bo-
" roughs and towns corporate, and all liber-
" ties and customs of the same, as to his
" highness shall be thought expedient, to
" the intent his majesty, at his grace's plea-
" sure, may duly erect, ordain, and make
" such and as many other boroughs and
" towns corporate within the said dominion,
" being more apt and convenient for that
" purpose,

" purpofe, and to endue them with fuch
" liberties and franchifes as to his moft ex-
" cellent wifdom fhall be thought neceffary
" for the wealth of the faid country *."

The well-known cafes alfo of the counties
of Chefter and Monmouth, and of the different fhires in the principality of Wales,
fully proves that in the reign of Henry VIII.
this principle was fufficiently underftood,
namely, that each diftrict had a right to
fend, if not a precife and accurate proportion
of reprefentatives to parliament, yet undoubtedly a fhare nearly equal to what it
could reafonably expect †. From thefe inftances

* Thirty-fourth of Henry VIII. c. 26, § 27. Thus it
appears that it was only *in virtue of this act* that the crown
was entitled to grant borough franchifes and liberties in
Wales.

† It will appear from the following ftate in what manner
the different counties in England were reprefented in the
reign of Edward I. and the additions which have been
fince made.

	Original number.	Added fince.	Total.
Bedfordfhire	4	—	4
Berks	6	3	9
Bucks	4	10	14
Cambridge	4	2	6

G   Cornwall

ftances alfo it appears, whatever powers the crown might affume, that it was reckoned the

	Original number.	Added fince.	Total.
Cornwall	14	30	44
Cumberland	4	2	6
Derby	4	—	4
Devonfhire	12	14	26
Dorfetfhire	12	8	20
Effex	4	4	8
Gloucefter	4	4	8
Hereford	6	2	8
Hertford	2	4	6
Huntingdon	4	—	4
Kent	6	12	18
Lancafhire	2	12	14
Leicefterfhire	4	—	4
Lincoln	6	6	12
Middlefex	6	2	8
Norfolk	8	4	12
Northamptonfhire	4	5	9
Northumberland	4	4	8
Nottinghamfhire	4	4	8
Oxford	4	5	9
Rutland	2	—	2
Shropfhire	6	6	12
Somerfetfhire	12	6	18
Southamptonfhire	8	18	26
Staffordfhire	4	6	10
Suffolk	6	10	16
Surrey	10	4	14
Suffex	16	12	28
Warwick	4	2	6
Weftmoreland	4	—	4

Wiltfhire

the safeft line to apply to the legiflature in
general for the grant of parliamentary privileges.

How then, it may be faid, do you account
for the prerogative affumed by the fovereign,
and acquiefced in by parliament, and by the
people, of granting legiflative privileges to
any place which the crown thought proper.

The fact feems to have been, that the
affumed prerogative of the crown in this
particular having originally been exercifed
in a very cautious manner, could give very
little offence,. and therefore remained un-
controuled by the defultory parliaments that
were affembled in former times; for which,
among other reafons, this may be affigned,
that though it was a privilege which many
places were defirous of poffeffing, yet it was

	Original number.	Added fince.	Total.
Wiltfhire	22	12	34
Worcefter	4	5	9
Yorkfhire	6	24	30

Chefter, Durham and Monmouth, had then no reprefentatives in the Englifh parliament. This table is drawn
up to prove that in the reign of Edward I. the reprefentation
was not fo unequal as it is at prefent, Yorkfhire and Lan-
cafhire only excepted.

in

in fact of a burdenfome nature. It was imagined, therefore, however defirous the crown
might be of extending it for its own purpofes, that the evil, in confequence of the
expence attending it; muft check itfelf.

It is impoffible to omit obferving what an
ungenerous advantage is taken by thofe who
are defirous of degrading the antiquity and
the power of parliaments, of fome inftances
which formerly occurred of boroughs having been inclined to diveft themfelves of
their parliamentary privileges. From this
circumftance it is pretended that parliaments
in former times had little weight in the
government of the ftate. Whereas thofe
privileges were confidered to be of fuch ef-
fential importance, that for one borough
that wifhed to be exempted, it will be found
that many were anxious to enjoy fo inefti-
mable a right, and when they were either
accidentally or purpofely neglected (as in
the well-known cafe of the borough of St.
Alban's) infifted legally for redrefs.

I muft differ alfo from the fentiment
which this writer feems to entertain refpecting

ing the confequences which would probably
refult from annihilating the parliamentary
privileges of certain boroughs to the amount
of one hundred reprefentatives. In confequence of fuch a reform, the crown would
doubtlefs be freed from the weight of fome
boroughs which have lately been employed
to give confiftency and firmnefs to the oppofition which it has received. But the confequence of always having a firm and fteady
phalanx to refift the meafures of the crown,
whether right or wrong, is, that a juft and
reafonable oppofition will find the people
become every day lefs inclined to fupport it.
Whereas, were oppofitions never to arife
without good grounds ; were they never to
difplay their banners but in cafes of urgent
neceffity ; were they founded not upon that
firmnefs and confiftency which depends
folely upon parliamentary intereft, but upon
the confidence which the people at large
have placed in great and illuftrious cha-
racters, (fuch an oppofition I mean as laft
war put the late Earl of Chatham at the
head of our affairs) how is it poffible to
fuppofe that an oppofition of this kind could
ever prove unfuccefsful ; more efpecially, if
the

the plan alluded to were to take place: for the boroughs over which the crown has an influence muſt always ſuffer more by the pruning knife of any political amputator, than thoſe in which reſpectable individuals, and their families, are ſuppoſed to enjoy a permanent, or what is called a natural intereſt.

If ſuch boroughs, however, are permitted to continue in their preſent ſtate, is it not natural to apprehend, that in a country ſo prone to luxury and expence as England has become, that it will not always be a juſt obſervation in reſpect to them, that they give conſiſtency and firmneſs to the ſpirit of independance. Already are they conſidered as a ſpecies of property, and as ſuch have been included in the rent-roll of an eſtate; their value and price in the market has been exactly aſcertained, and having once become a marketable commodity, why may not the crown become the purchaſer as well as a ſubject *. In that caſe, we ſhall feel all their inconveniencies without one ſingle ad-

* It is a point indeed pretty generally underſtood, that the crown has already put itſelf to no inconſiderable expence in purchaſing a dictatorial authority over ſome boroughs. A plan which might very eaſily be extended.

vantage.

vantage. Without even the confolation of
fuch fplendid talents, as they have formerly
tranfmitted to parliament, whofe luftre has
cheared many a gloomy theorift, brooding
over the calamities that muft befal a country,
one half of whofe legiflature can only boaft
of a few villagers for their conftituents.

Nay, if thefe boroughs continue in their
prefent ftate, and are preferved as a kind of
hot-bed or nurfery for the production of
parliamentary abilities, yet it is poffible that
our pofterity will have little reafon to re-
joice at the tendernefs we difplay. If many
men of genius are fent from them, is it not
too probable that they will quarrel about
the fhare which each of them ought to have
in the government of the ftate, that they
will range themfelves into different parties,
that each will aim by the common arts of a
demagogue to acquire power and popularity
to himfelf, and that the nation, diftracted
by the folly and madnefs of thofe who re-
prefent it, will not regret much the down-
fal of a fyftem of government fo prone to
confufion. The difplay of great eloquence,
and of great abilities, on fo diftinguifhed a
theatre as the fenate of a powerful nation,

may

may for fome time entertain the people; but they muft foon grow weary of an amufement, which experience has uniformly proved, the certain harbinger, of private mifery, and of public difafters.

The perufal of this Letter has certainly given rife to a variety of other thoughts, with which, however, I am not inclined to trouble either the author or the public; the fentiments of both are now ftated before a very impartial tribunal, though ftill of opinion, that fuch a plan of reform as is fketched out in the Lucubrations already alluded to, might be fafely adopted, yet, like him, I am defirous, if *a ftill fafer remedy*, that will fatisfy the wifhes of the people, can be carried into execution, to try how far it will be effectual. The time is certainly at laft arrived, when it is neceffary that *fomething fhould be done*; nor is it every flight prefcription that will renovate the vigour of a conftitution, finking under the weight of the moft dangerous maladies to which it can be fubjected.

F I N I S,

10793

9 7 8 3 3 3 7 2 2 4 6 2 2